Grandad was a very cle
He spent most of his time in his laboratory,
inventing things. I walked down the hall
and opened the laboratory door.

"Grandad!" I called out. "Are you in
here?" I could only see scientific equipment
and a big glass box in the laboratory.

"Here I am," said Grandad, appearing from behind the monstrous glass box. At the top of the glass box were green lights, clocks and plugs. "Are you enjoying your holiday?" he smiled.

"Yes, Grandad," I said. "But why is there a sign on the cupboard door under the stairs?"

Kirsty

Grandad

Theodore

ence
upboard.
Discover
ystery.

Grusilda xxx

Level 28

Entry Forbidden

I stared at the sign on the door to the cupboard under the stairs.

DO NOT ENTER.

That just made me want to open the door. The sign had not been there during my last holiday at Grandad's house.

Why was I forbidden to enter the cupboard? What could he have hidden behind that door?

I decided to ask him.

Grandad's smile disappeared. With a troubled look, he took off his glasses.

"You haven't been *inside* the cupboard, have you?" he asked.

"No," I replied. "But have you got a top-secret invention hidden in there?"

Grandad looked relieved. "No," he said. "It's just some old junk."

He put his glasses back on and his smile appeared again as if nothing had happened. "Now, Kirsty, I've got to finish this invention urgently. I'll see you at dinner time."

"OK," I said. But I wasn't convinced.

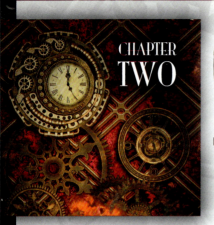

Only Old Junk?

I left Grandad to finish his glass-box invention and walked back past the cupboard door. But I was still curious about the old junk.

Shrugging my shoulders, I went upstairs to play a game on my smart phone. I told myself I wasn't interested in looking at old junk inside the cupboard.

The day passed without another thought about the forbidden cupboard.

After dinner that night, as I lay in bed, I started thinking about the cupboard again.

If there was only old junk inside, why had Grandad put a sign on the door? My mind began to imagine lots of weird things. What was really in there?

I couldn't sleep. I put on my dressing gown and slippers. I crept downstairs. Making my way silently along the hallway, I found myself in front of the mysterious cupboard.

Did I dare to open the door?

I reached out. My hand touched the cold door handle and I slowly turned it.

The door creaked open.

I gasped. There was *something* inside — and it definitely *wasn't* old junk.

Do Not Push!

Inside the forbidden cupboard was the most amazing sight. In front of me was a big glass box with glowing green lights, clocks and plugs.

It was exactly like the one I'd seen Grandad working on that morning. But why was he building *another* one?

I couldn't help myself. I knew I wasn't allowed. But I just had to go inside the cupboard!

There was a small door at the front of the glass box. Crouching down, I squeezed through the door. Once I was inside, I slowly looked around. In front of me I saw a large red button. Underneath the button, there was another one of Grandad's signs.

DO NOT PUSH!

Well, I'd already disobeyed one sign. And Grandad *had* said that there was only old junk in the cupboard. So I figured that nothing would happen.

I reached out. My finger lightly touched the button. I held my breath.

I pushed the button down ... hard! I waited. Nothing happened. Grandad was right after all. It really was just junk.

Now that I had seen the old junk for myself, I squeezed out of the glass box. I crept out of the cupboard, and back upstairs. As quietly as I could, I opened the door to my room. I was about to crawl into bed when, suddenly, I got a huge shock.

There was somebody else in my bed!

I crept back to the door to switch on the light. But, in my panic, I couldn't find the light switch.

Then, just as I was about to leave and wake up Grandad, *the person in the bed sat up!*

CHAPTER FOUR

A Strange Boy

"Who's there?" whispered a voice that sounded as terrified as I was. I peered into the darkness. My eyes slowly made out the shape of a boy, about the same age as me.

"Who are you? What are you doing here?" he demanded.

"Who are *you*? What are *you* doing here?" I shouted.

The boy stared at me furiously. I stared back, feeling even angrier.

And then he said something that made my head spin.

"This is *my* room!" he hissed. "You've made a dreadful mistake. Get out!"

His room? Had someone else come to stay with Grandad? Had he forgotten to tell me?

"What's your name?" he demanded.

I wasn't about to tell him my name first. "What's *your* name?" I asked the boy.

"Theodore Flannigan," he replied.

"Oh!" I gasped. "That's my grandad's name, too. Are you related to us?"

There was a flash as the boy struck a match. He lit a candle on the bedside table — a candle that hadn't been there before.

The candle spluttered and flickered. And then the light became brighter. Slowly, my eyes widened in the dim light.

I was amazed at what I saw.

CHAPTER FIVE

Where Am I?

The bed and the table were the same. But everything else was different. This wasn't my room. Somehow, I *had* made a dreadful mistake.

"I'm v-very s-sorry, Theodore" I stammered. "I must have been sleep-walking."

Theodore looked at me curiously. "Where did you come from?" he asked.

"From my grandad's house," I replied. "I live in the next suburb. I am staying for a short holiday."

Theodore looked even more curious. "What's a suburb?" he said.

Now this really was weird!

I opened the curtains to show him the street lights from outside. But there were none! No street lights, no houses, no shops, no buildings. All I could see was moonlight, shining onto empty fields.

"I must be dreaming," I muttered.

I pinched myself. Nothing happened. I was still in a strange house with a boy who had the same name as my grandad.

Suddenly, I thought about the strange glass box. What *had* it done?

"We need to go downstairs," I said to Theodore. "I need to show you something."

Together, we made our way to the cupboard under the stairs. I reached out and slowly turned the handle. The door creaked open. I gasped.

The glass box was gone!

Theodore peeked in the door. "What were you looking for?" he asked.

It was time to find out what was going on. Maybe the machine had transported me or sent me to sleep for a long time.

"Where am I?" I asked. "And what day is it?"

"You're at *my* house," said the boy. "And it's August 17th."

I breathed a sigh of relief. At least it was still the same day.

"In the year 1938," said Theodore.

I couldn't believe what I had heard. Could the strange glass box have taken me back in time? Then I had another thought. If the box had taken me back in time, was *this* Theodore Flannigan my grandfather?

We crept back upstairs and sat on the side of the bed. I could hardly think straight. Theodore yawned.

"I'm tired," he said. "Let's work out what to do in the morning. You can sleep in my bed," he added. "I'll sleep on the floor."

I couldn't sleep. I was wide awake. After an hour, I heard a stair creak. I sat up, my eyes wide open. If someone discovered me, I would be in big trouble. Who would believe my story?

I heard the door handle turn slowly. The door creaked open. I hid under the blankets.

"Kirsty," said the voice. "Kirsty, are you there?"

It was my grandad. I was happy yet terrified at the same time. I raced across the room. Grandad put a finger on his lips.

"Not a sound," he said. "The boy *must not* wake."

We sneaked downstairs. Grandad led me past the forbidden cupboard and into his laboratory.

Only it wasn't his laboratory any more. It was an old store room, full of vegetables, seeds and garden tools. In the centre of the room was the new glass machine that he had been working on the day before.

"Get inside, quickly!" said Grandad.

I hurried in, and he squeezed in beside me. He pressed a large red button, just like the one I never should have touched in the other glass box. Nothing happened. I groaned.

"Don't worry," said Grandad, smiling.

"My chronomobile travels so fast, you don't even notice. We're back," he said. "We're safe again. *You're* safe again."

And we were. We crawled out of the glass box. I climbed wearily up the stairs to my room and looked around. Everything was just as I had left it. I flopped into bed, exhausted.

"I'll explain everything in the morning," came Grandad's voice from downstairs.

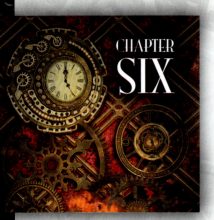

CHAPTER SIX

Dream or Reality?

The next morning, I joined Grandad for breakfast. I waited for him to explain everything but, curiously, he didn't. He just drank his tea and read the newspaper.

Then he looked up at me, as if nothing had happened.

"What's the matter, Kirsty?" he asked. "You look tired. Too many dreams last night?"

I gazed at Grandad closely. Was he pretending – or had he really forgotten our adventure?

He didn't say another word. He just finished his cup of tea and gave me a mysterious smile.

"Well, it's time to start work," he said.

Grandad was not acting at all like someone who had just rescued his granddaughter from a time-travelling adventure. I started to wonder whether I really *had* dreamt it all. I felt very strange.

Grandad folded his newspaper under his arm, turned around and gave me a big wink.

"Isn't it strange how *real* some dreams seem?" he said with an even more mysterious smile. "It's almost like they actually happened."

I nodded. "Yes it is, Grandad!"

I suppose it is very hard to tell the difference between a dream and reality ... sometimes!